# Google Classroom

## *An Easy Google Classroom Guide To Take Your Classroom Digital*

# Table of Contents

# Introduction

Google Classroom is going to change the face of education. For years, teachers have spent so much of their time both inside and outside of the classroom, trying to find the best way to educate their students and provide feedback promptly. In addition to spending time in the classroom going through their lesson plans, they also were in charge of copying materials, grading papers and essays, administering tests. All of these took a long time to accomplish and could cut into the learning time for the students. Sometimes, to save time, teachers would pick the easiest options for learning, cutting out creativity and some of the fun in learning.

The hardships were not just on the teacher. Students often had to keep track of papers from different classes and in the clutter they may miss out on important announcements or information about the assignments. Asking questions both inside and outside of class could be a chore as reaching teachers was not always the easiest. And while the teacher was busy trying to organize their lesson plans or finding time to grade papers, the students were missing out on valuable learning time.

Google Classroom is a free platform that can make education better for both the teacher and the students. Teachers can have all their classes in one place, assign homework and send announcements and save a lot of time. Students can always be up to date on their work, receive feedback on their assignments, and even reach their teacher in real time. It is a win-win for both parties and can make learning fun and enjoyable again.

This guidebook is going to provide you with the information you need to get started with Google Classroom. We start out with some of the basics of Classroom and then move into some of the different tasks that teachers can do and some of the different tasks that students can take advantage of. Finishing up with some of the best tips of how to use Classroom, this guidebook will help you to see all the great features and get started on using this application on your schedule.

With all the options for educational platforms available to use, Google Classroom is leading the pack with easy apps that many already enjoy and all the available features that you can use for free. Check out this guidebook before getting started and learn just how amazing this platform can be.

# Chapter 1: What is Google Classroom?

Google Classroom is a new tool that teachers and students can use in an educational setting. It blends the different apps from Google to help schools in their goal of education. Teachers can create a classroom and invite all their students to join. During the year, homework assignments, discussion questions, and even testing can be completed on the Google Classroom platform, making it easier for students to complete their work even outside the classroom.

This platform has several different uses. Many teachers who conduct online classes have turned to using Google Classroom because it allows them to easily post up reading material and assignments as well as the required class participation (discussions) and other information that the students need. Since most students can use Google and the platform is free, this is a great way to get online courses started.

Regular classrooms that meet each day can use this information as well. Students inside the classroom can take tests through the platform, get together in groups and answer questions for discussion, and even submit answers all in one place. When the teacher assigns homework, it will be waiting on the platform for the students once they get home.

Google Classroom is a great way to make education more fun and to take out some of the hassles that slow down learning in the classroom. Students can easily use this platform to ask their questions or to complete assignments, and there is no need to waste time printing out packets for each student or handing out assignments in the classroom. Everything is in one place so the students can spend more time learning!

# The Basics of Google Classroom

The great thing about Google Classroom is that it ties together many of the other products from Google to provide a paperless system for educational institutions to use. You will be able to use Google Drive to create and distribute assignments, and Gmail is good for sending information to the students. Google Calendar helps the students know when different assignments are due and even when other important events, such as tests, will occur. Get class can also use Google Docs to submit assignments and the teacher can then view and grade the homework.

All of these work together to make things easier for students and teachers. Communication is done just through regular emails and it takes just a few seconds for the teacher to create assignments and for students to submit their work. Also, Google Classroom does not use ads in the program so no one has to worry about this interfering with the work or about Google collecting private information.

## Assignments

Google Drive is going to be the main point of contact for assignments with Google Classroom. Teachers can either look at documents the students have uploaded, and grade from there, or they can upload a template that each student can change and resubmit as their own. This can be helpful if the teacher needs a worksheet or discussion questions answered for homework. Also, if the student needs to attach supporting documents, this can easily be done in Google Drive as well.

## Grading

Teachers can choose the way that they would like to grade in this platform. One option is just to have the students submit the work and teachers can choose to grade by marking answers correct or not before sending the information back. On other assignments, such as projects that will take some time or for essays, the teacher can track progress, make edits, and even grade with notes and send it back for revisions.

There are several applications that can assist with this grading option as well. Flubaroo is perfect if you have worksheets or multiple choice tests that simply need to be graded. This application can take the assignment, grade it automatically, and then send the grade to the students so they get feedback right away, even when the teacher is busy.

## Communication

Most of the communication can be done through Gmail. Teachers can send announcements, homework assignments, and other information to students and the students can send questions and information back to the teacher when it is most convenient for them. Gmail is easy to use, and it only takes a few minutes for students to create their accounts if they don't already have one.

In addition to using Gmail, Google Drive and YouTube can be used for communications. Teachers can post to Google Drive the new assignments and announcements the students need and YouTube can be great for sending video and other media when it pertains to the classroom.

## Time-cost

First, the cost. This platform is free to use, both for the teacher and the students. The teacher simply needs to create their classroom and then send the code to their students. This allows the students to get into the classroom, access any announcements and assignments, and even to ask their questions. The classroom is secure, so only those invited can see what is inside, and since Google doesn't allow advertisements, parents know that it is safe.

Next, the amount of time that teachers can save using this platform is immense. They can add on applications that grade worksheets and homework automatically for them. They won't have to waste time at the copy machine or handing out papers to all the students. They can spend their class time teaching and save the announcements and homework assignments for later.

**Mobile Version**

Google has also made a mobile version of Classroom that allows for even more features including the ability to snap photos and add them to assignments, share other apps including web pages, PDF's, and images, and the ability to get their homework assignments even when they aren't around an internet connection. This is available for both Android and iPhone products, making it easier for everyone to use.

Google Classroom is designed to make education easier. Teachers can spend more time interacting with their students and less time worrying about all the paperwork while students can easily get to their important announcements and upload homework assignments on their time. With the ability to work on many of the popular Google apps, this is one of the best free platforms to help with education.

# Benefits of Google Classroom

In the modern world, there are many similar platforms that promise to deliver success. Google Classroom has many great benefits that the other platforms lack including:

- Easy to setup—the setup for Google Classroom only takes a few minutes. The teacher simply needs to set up their class, invite their students and anyone else they wish, and then share their information including questions, announcements, and questions when needed.
- Less paper and time—instead of teachers making twenty or more copies of each worksheet or handing out packets of papers for discussions, reading, and tests, all of the work is now online. This can save a lot of paper and makes student management easier.
- Easy organization—students can join their classroom and see all the assignments in their Work page or on the calendar. The materials needed for the class, such as reading materials, worksheets, and discussion questions, will be located in their Google Drive folder.
- Enhanced communication—inside Google Classroom, the teacher will be able to release announcements and create assignments. For homework or online classes, discussions can begin in real time. The students can share their resources and interact, even if they are not in the same room.
- Works with other apps—Google Classroom will work with the other Google apps like Forms, Drive, Gmail, Calendar, and Docs, making it easier than ever to complete assignments.
- Secure and affordable—since this is from Google, the app allows you to keep all of your information secure. There are no advertisements that get in the way, and Google does not use this information to sell advertising space. This makes it secure for students to use. Also, using Google Classrooms is free!

While there are other platforms out there that can help schools with education, Google has many great (and free!) apps that combine to make Google Classroom. Since many students are already using these apps and have a Gmail account, or can create one quickly, it is an efficient way to share information between the teacher and the students. Whether the class takes place in person or completely online, this is a great resource to save paper, help students get questions answered, and to even promote discussions outside of the classroom.

# Chapter 2: Getting Started for Teachers

Google Classroom is going to make things much easier for teachers. Many teachers are frustrated by the time wasted in the classroom, passing out papers, grading essays and trying to give feedback. Google Classroom can make this easier in so many ways! Let's explore how Google Classroom is going to transform the way that teachers work so that they can spend more time with the students and less time with all that paperwork!

## Setting Up the Classroom

Setting up your classroom is going to be easier than you think. While a lot of other learning platforms ask you to jump through hoops and learn a lot of different tabs before getting to use the system, Google Classroom tries to keep it simple. Some of the things that you need to do to start with Classroom include:

1. Visit classroom.google.com. You will be able to sign up for your account in this part, using your school email address to login. If your school administrator has some special rules about which emails to use, you will need to talk to them.
2. Click the "+" that is located on the right on top of the page. This allows you to create the first class. Click "Create class."
3. Name the class so that it is easy to remember. Consider not only the name of the class but also the section. This is important if you are teaching more than one section of the same class. You can say something like Senior English: Period 2. Name the class anything you want, just think about how you will recognize them later.
4. Now that the class is created, your students can join it. You can send the link to the students in your class to ensure they get into

the right section. While waiting for students to join, be a bit creative. Change up the theme to make it match the course name or just to something you like.

5. Don't forget to fill out the "About" section. This is going to be useful to students before starting your class because it gives them some information about the course. Place information such as your email, the syllabus, grading scale, and other information that the students may need through the year.

# Daily Use of Classroom

Once your Classroom is set up and students star to join, it is up to you to have fun with the layout and make the platform work with you. There are some things that you can do with this platform to help students learn including:

- Make announcements—this helps you communicate with the whole class. Simply click on the "Announcement" button and then write the message you want them to do. It is possible to provide links, YouTube videos, and files from your Google Drive to the announcement if needed.
- Add assignments—following the same idea as announcements; you can create a new assignment. Simply write out the name of the assignment, a short description, and attach any files that are necessary. Make sure to add the due date so students can prepare.
- Manage students—to manage your students, go to the "Students" tab. From here, you can allow students to comment, post and comment, or just to read the material. You can send emails to one or two students at a time, and even remove them from the class if they end up switching.
- Grading assignments—after the assignment due date is up, you can click on a student's name to see the files attached. You can then click on "No Grade" and then place the grade that you want to give them. If the system automatically graded a student based on your settings, you can always go back in and change the

grade. Make sure to hit "Return" when done to make the changes.

**Things Classroom Doesn't Do**

Google Classroom has a lot of great features and can make teaching a bit easier, but there are a few things that it is not able to do for teachers. Luckily, with just a bit of work on your part and using the tools that Google provides, it is still possible to finish these tasks and get them to the students without too much hassle. Some of the things that Classroom is not able to do include:

- Provide quizzes and tests—while you can send quizzes and tests as assignments through Classroom, this platform will not create them for you. Using Google Forms, you can create the test and then send a link to your assignments. With the help of Flubaroo, the quizzes are graded for you, but all of this will be outside Google Classroom.
- Chat—as of right now, Classroom does not have a chat feature. You can use other Google Apps to chat or rely on email to communicate.
- Full-featured Forums—the forum feature is not present in this platform, but you can use Forms and Drive to start discussions in your class.

With most of these disadvantages, there are ways to work around them so you can still get all the features you want, you just need to utilize the various apps that Google provides.

# What Else Can I do with Google Classroom?

There is so much that you can do with this Google platform! Whether you want to move your whole class online and spend time in class learning and having fun, or you just want to place homework assignments online so students don't misplace them, Google Classroom is the answer you need.

## Better Organization

When taking care of twenty or more students, it is easy to become disorganized and misplace things. If you have more than one class, the disorganization can get really bad. Classroom makes this easier by separating each class out, allowing you to set individual due dates, and having your students place their homework all in one place. Some ways that Classroom helps keep teachers organized include:

- The student will be able to place their work in one folder where the teacher can access it from Google Drive. The teacher will then be able to give feedback or show grades in the same place.
- Homework collection is all done in one place. Depending on the assignment, the teacher can even provide feedback while the student is working on it.
- Less time on administrative tasks means the teacher can spend time answering questions and teaching.
- The ability to choose if a document can be edited or only viewed.
- Anytime the teacher needs to post an assignment, question, or announcement; the Classroom will send it to every student. This saves time compared to sending information out to each student.
- The ability to send messages to individual students as well. If you need to notify one or two students about a meeting or homework assignment, it is possible without notifying the whole class.

Organization can be a teachers' best friend. It allows them to think clearly, have more time for students, and get the work done on time. Google Classroom can make staying organized easier than ever.

## Work Is Easier

Everyone likes it when their work is easier, and Google Classroom can make this happen. It is easy to use; if you already know how to use a few Google apps, you are set for becoming an expert with Classroom. Classroom allows teachers to assess how their students are doing, connect with the whole class or individual students and even monitor how students are doing all while attending other work. Some of the great things that you can do with Classroom to make your work easier include:

- Teachers in the same district can be on different domains while still sharing content and files together. If you know, a teacher in the district that has a workbook you like or you both want to connect your students together; this can happen through Classroom.
- The reuse feature allows you to reuse any of the information that you have used before including questions, assignments, and announcements. For example, if you teach the same class again the second semester, you use have the reuse feature to place assignments back up.
- Classroom is easy to set up. Once your district signs up, you just need to use your assigned email and set up the classes that you want. Prepare everything that is needed in one area to share with your students.
- Everything is paperless. No more handing out papers, standing in line for the copy machine, or worrying about students losing assignments. Everyone in your class can log on and get to work.
- Classroom is very accessible, available through tablets, PC's, laptops, and now even on some smartphones.
- If you are planning on going on vacation, you can plan it all out ahead of time, scheduling assignments and other announcements before you leave. The platform will send you an email when the posts go live, and your substitutes can stay on schedule even when you're not there.

# Grading Process

Grading papers, assignments, and tests can take hours of a teachers' time. The more classes you take on, the longer the grading process can take. While teachers want to give each student the attention they deserve, they also have to prepare for classes and keep up with home life as well. Classroom can help to make the grading process easier, helping students to get faster results and freeing up time for the teacher. Classroom can help by:

- Making it easier to grade. The teacher will be able to pull up a spreadsheet and add in the grades as well as any feedback. Once you press the "Return" button, the students will be able to see their grades.
- Making it easier to monitor students once they have completed assignments. The teacher can also give feedback and grade them right away.
- Making it easy to see who has and hasn't turned in their assignments.
- Offering options for grading students. They can choose from a numerical value already in the system or create their value. Students will be able to see the grades once they are imported.
- Allowing for instant grading. There are add-ons to the program that allow for instant grading. For worksheets and multiple choice options, these add-ons can take care of the grading and free up time.

# Communication

There are many times when teachers and students will need to communicate, and Classroom can make this easier than ever. Teachers will be able to make announcements, send out assignments, and provide feedback to the students. And students will have the opportunity to ask questions when needed. Some of the things you can do with Classroom for open communication include:

- Opening up a question and answer portion. This allows for more discussion both inside and outside the class.
- Teachers can use a "Create a Question" feature to start the discussion. Use this for polls and surveys to see how well the students understand the topic.
- Post topics and questions to start an online discussion. This can be used during class for small group discussions or for homework to get students thinking and communicating about the reading.
- Emailing can help with asking questions, sending reminders (especially during long breaks), and getting other information out to students.
- Discussions can help students to understand the material more and opens up students who may be shy and less likely to discuss during class.

**Becoming More Creative**

Sometimes, your classroom will need a bit more creativity to get the point across. While math topics may be fine with just adding worksheets and tests on Classroom, others like English and Science can allow for some more creativity. Classroom makes it easier to change things up to facilitate different learning styles to make education more fun. Some of the things you can do to change up learning through in Classroom include:

- Work on discussions. This can help everyone participate in class, even those who may be too shy in class to speak up.
- Multi-media is easy to use in Classroom. Bring in YouTube videos, pictures from online, or anything else that can supplement your lessons.
- Create your games. Have students compete to answer questions, create your own learning board game, or find some great options online to fit your topics.
- Offer different project options. While some people may like to create a poster or write an essay, others may be better at

performances, speaking, or singing. These can all be done and uploaded on Classroom as well.

Creativity makes the classroom so much better and can allow for more learning than you will find with just using a textbook. Google Classroom allows you to try out different types of learning materials without adding to your workload.

Classroom is one of the best tools that teachers can use to make life easier. Rather than spending so much time on administrative tasks like making copies, finding new tests, and grading, Classroom allows everything to be in one place. Add in the benefits of using different learning materials, and Classroom will change the way students learn.

# Chapter 3: Getting Started for Students

Teachers and educators can get quite a bit out of Google Classroom to organize their students and make their teaching more effective. They are allowed to monitor all of their students in one area, keeping classes separate, making announcements, and doing so much more to help students learn so they can spend more time teaching rather than spending so much time on their regular administrative tasks.

Students can also benefit from Google Classroom. While the students will not be able to add people to the class and are limited on the resources they can upload onto the platform, there are plenty of opportunities for them to interact with each other, communicate with the teacher, and learn in new ways!

**Logging In**

At the beginning of the school year, your teacher will be able to invite you to join their classroom. You will simply need to give them a preferred email and then accept the invitation and link that they send to you later on. This will allow you access to the classroom, and you can see all the announcements and assignments that the teacher gives for that year. You can also stream content, read materials, take tests and quizzes, partake in discussions, and hand in homework assignments all in one place.

Make sure that the email address you provide is one you use often. Otherwise, you could miss out on some of the important information needed to do well in class. Consider signing up for a Gmail account that is only for school and giving that to each teacher who uses Google Classroom. This allows all your school announcements to be in one place and limits the chance that something gets lost in another email address.

**Sharing**

Students are allowed to share their thoughts and opinions on Classroom. Going to the Stream tab, you can provide an answer to discussion questions the teacher posts, and the whole class will be able to see. You can attach supporting documents to this as well including videos, web links, files, and documents.

This is separate from where you would do tests or essays and other homework. The Stream tab is a place where others will be able to see your information, what you have posted, and can even comment on it themselves. If you are doing a discussion question or you have found something interesting to share with the whole class, this is the option for you. If you are sending in a homework assignment or a test, you will use Google Forms or Drive to get this done.

**Assignments**

Your teacher will be able to upload assignments onto Classroom for everyone to see. Rather than printing off papers and expecting a student to remember each assignment from multiple classes each day, Classroom allows the student to get into their class and find all the information needed for the assignment. To see your assignments, you simply need to click on the button to "View All" and see a list of assignments for a particular class. You can see To-Do items, such as if you need to read a document before starting, or a reminder for a test and students have the option to mark whether an assignment is done.

Many assignments will require a link or file to complete. For example, if a student needed to write out an essay or submit answers to a discussion question, they may have written the answers in Word outside of Classroom. In these cases, the assignment feature allows students to upload these links. Students can also make a comment about an assignment, but remember that others in the class will be able to see these comments.

If a student has a question about an assignment, they can simply email the teacher through their Gmail account. The teacher can then respond personally to the student, without notifying the whole class, and get the questions answered promptly.

## Organization

Classroom is hooked up to Google Calendar so students can look at their assignments, test dates, and other important information and find out when everything is due at a glance. This can help students to keep track of their assignments and makes it easier to plan out how to get all the work done. In Calendar, students can change the color to match with the class, and they can set up text message alerts to remind them of upcoming due dates on assignments.

## Feedback

Google Classroom allows students to discuss various parts of their homework and tests with the teacher. In a regular classroom setting, the student will submit the work, the teacher will grade it with a few comments, and that is the end. There isn't enough time in class for the student to discuss the grade or comment and many may not be able to bring up this discussion later. With Classroom, the student can leave a comment under feedback from the teacher, and a discussion can begin that helps the student understand why they got a certain grade or even clarify their answers. This allows for more discussion and learning than what may go on in the traditional classroom.

## Discussion Time

Many teachers like the feature of adding discussion questions inside Classroom. These discussion questions allow students to talk about a particular topic and learn together in a setting that is more comfortable than speaking in the classroom. Sometimes the teacher may not have time for a full discussion in class and other times; this is a tool used to bring shy students out to speak their opinions. Either way, students are learning from each other, considering different ideas, and gaining more knowledge in an easy way.

## Google Apps

Google has many great apps to use, and all of them are free. This makes it easy for students to get on and use everything that is needed on the platform. Through Google Classroom, students can enjoy other apps including Google Calendar, Google Spreadsheets, Docs, Presentation, Gmail, Drive, and much more. These are great tools that can help students out at any level of education, even if their class is not using Classroom at the time. Students will become familiar with using these apps on the platform and seeing what a difference they make in learning and presenting themselves.

## Other Functions and Benefits of Classroom

There are so many great benefits to students for using Google Classroom. While many times the focus is on the teacher and how they will be able to streamline their teaching process and help students learn more, students are getting some of the best benefits out of this tool. They are opening up to new ideas, finding creative ways to learn, and even having more teacher attention than in a traditional classroom.

Some of the other benefits that students can enjoy using Classroom include:

- If a particular lesson is not clear to the student, they can add feedback and save the lesson to a new folder for revisions later once clarification is met.
- Students can privately ask their teacher a question
- The ability to create and also monitor how they are doing in a particular class using Google Sheets.
- Ability to email either individual students or a group of students and start up a conversation. This can be helpful in discussions when missing a day in school, or for a project.
- Students can submit their assignments as attachments in many forms including links, videos, files, and voice clips.
- Reduce how much paper is used in the classroom.
- Fewer missed due dates since they have all their homework in one place and can monitor on Google Calendar at a glance.
- Students who are shy can reply to questions online and engage without being worried about talking in front of other people. This allows for more engagement out of the class and for everyone to be heard.
- Classroom is flexible, easy to access, and both instructors and students can receive benefits of using it.
- While Classroom is only available for students who attend an educational institution which using the platform, all of the Google apps are available to everyone for free, allowing students and individuals to get the benefits of these apps, even if they aren't in class.
- Students can use Google Classroom on their smartphones, making it easier to receive notifications and work on assignments anywhere.

- It is easy for students to work together, even outside of class, and for teachers to provide feedback and comments on assignments so students learn more than ever.

- Better organization—students can keep all the information for one class in one place. This limits how the likelihood of losing an assignment, forgetting about it or leaving the paper at home.

Students can simply log on to their classroom and complete homework assignments, tests, and more in one location.

- Instant feedback—taking tests can be hard, but it is nice to get instant feedback. Your teacher can choose an add-on that provides instant feedback on test scores and some types of homework, allowing you a chance to see how you did right away rather than waiting a week or more for the teacher to have time to grade all the papers.

Google Classroom is a great learning companion for students. There are many great (and free!) apps that students may already know how to use. It facilitates different types of learning, allows even the quietest student in the class to speak up and be heard, and can help provide instant feedback and more discussion between students and teachers to help the student learn more than they can in a traditional classroom. While teachers may love how Classroom helps them to be more effective at their jobs, students will enjoy how easy it makes the learning process and all the options it opens up in the class.

# Chapter 4: Tips and Tricks to Get the Most out of Google Classroom

Both teachers and students can benefit from Google Classroom. It is an easy platform that brings together some of the best apps that Google has to offer to help teachers get the most out of their lectures and students to learn in new and exciting ways. Here we will look at some of the tips and tricks that both students and teachers can try to get the most out of the Google Classroom platform.

## Tips for Teachers

### Tip 1: Learn all the ways to give feedback.

Your students are going to thrive with as much feedback as you can provide them and Classroom offers you many options for this. You can leave comments on assignments that students hand in, on the file that is submitted, through email, and so much more. Consider the best places to leave feedback and let your students know so they can be on the lookout for ways to improve.

Some of the ways that you can utilize comments include:

- Class comments—you can do this by starting a common for the whole class on the outside of the assignment or in the announcement. This is going to be a comment that the whole class is going to see so don't use it if you just want to talk to the individual student. It is a good option to use if you want to answer a question that a lot of people have.
- Private comments—you can do this by going into the file of an individual student. You will be able to see the submissions this

student has made and can click on the comment bar near the bottom. When you add a comment, the student will be the only one who can see it.

- Comments to media—you can do this by clicking on the file that the student submitted to you. Highlight the area and then comment on that particular part of the project. This can help you to show an example of the student or explain your thoughts and how something needs to be changed.

## Tip 2: Use the description feature

When creating an assignment, make sure to add a nice long description. This is where you explain what the assignment is all about, how to complete it, and even when the assignment is due. Often students are juggling many classes all at once and by the time they get to the assignment, they have forgotten all the instructions you gave them in class. Or if a student missed class that day, the description can help them understand what they missed. A good description can help to limit emails with questions and can help students get started on the assignment without confusion.

## Tip 3: Use Flubaroo

Grading can take up a lot of your time, especially when dealing with many students and multiple classes. You want to provide your students with accurate feedback as quickly as possible, but traditional teaching can make this impossible. Add-ons like Flubaroo can make this easier. When creating a quiz or test, you can use Flubaroo so that when a student submits their answers, the app will check them and provide a score right away. The student can see how well they did on the quiz and where they may need to make some changes.

This kind of add-on is best for things such as multiple choice assignments and tests. It allows the student to see what they understand right away without having to wait for the teacher to correct everything. You are able to go back and change the grade on a particular assignment if the add-on grades incorrectly, you want to add bonus points, or for some other reason.

If you are creating assignments like discussion posts, opinions, projects, and essays, Flubaroo is not the best option for you. This app is not going to understand how to grade these projects and since each one is more creative and doesn't necessarily have a right or wrong answer, it is important for the teacher to go in and grade. There are many places where you can provide feedback, even at various points of the project, to help the student make changes before the final grade.

**Tip 4: Reuse some of your old posts**

At times, you may have an assignment, question, or announcement that is similar to something you have posted before. For example, if you have a weekly reading or discussion assignment that is pretty much the same every week, you will be able to use the reuse option on Classroom. To do this, just click on the "+" button that is on the bottom right of the screen. You will then be able to select "Reuse post." Pick from a list of options that you already used for the class. If there are any modifications, such as a different due date, you can make those before posting again. When reusing the post, you have the option to create new copies of the attachments that were used in the original posting.

**Tip 5: Share your links and resources**

There may be times that you find an interesting document, video, or other media that you would like your students to see. Or they may need resources for an upcoming project, and you want to make it easier for them to find. In this case, you should use the announcement feature. This allows all the important documents to be listed right at the top of the classroom rather than potentially getting lost further down in assignments.

This is a great tip to use for items of interest that you would like to share with your students or for documents and files that they will need right away. If you have a resource that the students will need throughout the year, you should place it into the "About" tab to prevent it getting lost as the year goes on.

# Tips for Students

### Tip 1: Pick one email for all of your classes

Consider having a dedicated email that is for all of your classes. You don't need to separate it and have an email for each of your classes, but create a new email that will only accept information from all classes using Google Classroom. Whenever a teacher announces they use this platform, you will use this email. This helps you to keep all of your classes in one place and can prevent you from missing out on your announcements and assignments because they got lost in all your personal emails.

### Tip 2: Check your classes daily

As the year goes on, your teacher will probably get into a routine of when they make posts, and you can check the class at that time. But it is still a good idea to stay on top of a class and check it each day. You never know when you may forget about an assignment that is almost due or when the teacher will add an extra announcement for the whole class. If you only check your classes on occasion, you could miss out on a lot of important information along the way. Check in daily to stay up to date and to get everything in on time.

## Tip 3: Look at the calendar

One of the first places you should go when opening up to a class is the Calendar. This is going to list everything important that is coming your way in the next few months (updated as the teacher adds new announcements and assignments) so you can plan out your time. For some students, it is easier to get a grasp on the work when it is in table form rather than just looking at a date in the announcements. Use this as a planning tool and check it often to see if there is anything new to add to your schedule.

## Tip 4: Ask questions for clarification

Classroom makes it easier for students to ask the questions they need before starting an assignment. In some classrooms, it can be hard to find time to ask a question. When twenty or more students are asking questions at the same time, or the teacher runs out of time and barely gets the assignment out before the next bell, there are many students who may leave the classroom without any clue how to begin on an assignment.

With Classroom, the students can ask any questions they have when it is convenient. If they have a question about an assignment, they can comment on the assignment or send an email. If they have a question about some feedback that is left for a test, discussion, or essay, they can ask it right on the assignment. Classroom has opened up many options for talking to your teacher and getting your questions answered so don't be shy and sit in the dark when you need clarification.

## Tip 5: Learn about all the features of Google

Google has many great features that both students and teachers can take advantage of. Many people don't realize all of the different apps that are available on Google, and since these apps can be used together with Classroom and are free, it is important to take advantage of as many as possible. Some of the best Google products that can help with learning include:

- Gmail—Gmail makes it easier for students and teachers to communicate about the class without sharing the information with other students.
- Calendar—students will be able to see at a glance when important assignments, tests, and other information occurs in their class.
- Drive—Drive is a great place to put all assignments, questions, and other documents that are needed to keep up in class. Teachers can place learning materials and assignments inside for the student to see and students can submit their assignments all in one place.
- YouTube—students are used to spending time on YouTube, and teachers can use this to their advantage to find educational videos for their class. Students can either look at links that the teacher provides or search for their videos.
- Docs—this program works similar to Microsoft Word, but since it is free, it can be nice for those students who don't already have Word at home. Students can write, edit, and make changes just like on regular documents and then submit back to the teacher.
- Google Earth/Maps—explore the world around us with these two great features. Google Earth lets students learn more about the world by allowing them to look up different areas and see them from an actual satellite. Google Maps can help with Geography around the world or students can even create their Maps with this program.

These are just a few of the different apps available with Google that can make a difference in the way that students learn. While not all of them will apply to every class, a good understanding of each can help the teacher pick the right one for their class and helps the student learn as much as possible.

## Tip 6: Don't forget about tests and quizzes


Sometimes, a teacher may give you a few days to complete a test at home if there isn't enough time to do everything in the classroom. This gives you a bit of freedom to study for longer and fit the test around your schedule, but when a test isn't due right away, it is sometimes easy to forget about it. Make sure to watch your Calendar and set up announcements to remind yourself that an important assignment or test is due.


The issue with forgetting about some of these things is that with the right add-ons, the system may grade the test as incomplete or give you a zero (if the test is multiple choice). The teacher may be willing to go back in and fix the grade or extend the due date if you talk to them, but it is still better to just get the test done in the first place. This shows that you can adhere to deadlines and saves some time for your teacher.


Google Classroom may seem like a simple platform, but there is just so much that you can do with it both as a teacher and as a student. The options for learning, sending information back and forth, and all the organization and freedom now available in the classroom can make this an attractive choice for many schools.

# Chapter 5: New Features of Google Classroom

As Google Classroom has enjoyed more widespread use, new features and benefits have come out. These are meant to make it easier for both teachers and students to get more out of this platform and for them to find it easier to use. Some of the most recent updates to Classroom include:

1. Quizlet Class—with this update, the teacher can create a quizlet at the same time they create the class. Once the account is set up, you can set up the Quizlet account and link both of these together. When students join the class, Quizlet will notify them at the same time.

2. Upload playing tests—this one is useful for music classes. Students will be able to record playing tests or upload one they have already done. The teacher can then view the playing test and leave their feedback. Students can choose to listen to the test again to make improvements or ask questions if something doesn't make sense to them.

3. Outside of class viewing party—there are many live events that can help with a particular topic, but which may be hard to take the whole class too. For example, live performances, debates, speeches, and even movies could help the teacher talk about certain points. If these live events happen after class hours, the teacher can incorporate them into the class and add live posts and discussions to keep students working together.

4. Warm up questions—if the teacher would like to assess how well students understood the class or perhaps do a quick review before a test, the warm up question feature can help. Post the questions and let students either put in an essay answer or multiple choice. This feature doesn't allow students to see other answers so you know how each one thinks without influence from their peers.

5. Flubaroo—this is a great add-on that allows some homework assignments and tests to be graded immediately. Assignments that use multiple choice questions and true and false statements will enjoy Flubaroo because students can submit the work and receive feedback right away. This saves time for the teacher, allows students to see which questions they got wrong, and speeds up the learning process.

6. Class discussions—one cool feature of Classroom is the ability to have several classes talk together. Teachers can connect with other teachers in the same, or similar classes and students can share ideas and discussions.

7. Photo assignments—Classroom can even be used on a smartphone and tablet so students can use their cameras to complete projects. Send students on a scavenger hunt, let them upload a picture of their homework, or use the camera in another way.

8. Forums—Forums are another way to expand on the class discussion, making it easy for a whole grade level to converse together and share their knowledge. The school can set up several teachers and administrators to watch the comments of the whole school. Younger students can ask questions about which classes to take, for example, and older students can find out about colleges, how their credits work, and so on.

9. Poll questions—all teachers can use a poll question, but it works particularly well for math teachers. They can turn a math problem into a poll so that students can use the skills they learn in class to come up with an answer. This feature also works well for teachers to gather feedback.

10. Guided reading—test vocabulary, have students answer questions as they get through parts of a reading assignment, and help make sure important concepts are understood by the whole class before moving on.

11. Post a link—posting links can bring in outside sources for students to learn even more. The teacher can add in digital resources and videos.

12. Parent support—Google has added a feature that allows teachers to communicate with and keep parents up to date on student progress. The parents will need to sign up for the class and then will receive a weekly update and email digests so that

they can keep track of upcoming assignments, all important announcements, and how well their student is doing in class. This makes it easier for parents to participate in learning without taking up valuable teacher time.

13. Teacher control—teachers, have full control over the classroom. They will be able to decide when something is appropriate and may need to ooGstep in if comments don't stay on topic or students begin to attack each other. Classroom has made this easy for the teacher to control what is going on at all times.


As time goes on, Google Classroom will add on more great features that make it easier for teachers and students to work together inside and outside the classroom. Teachers can already enjoy the ability to be in charge of the Classroom, posting important announcements, handing out assignments without wasting time and paper, and communicating with students. Students will enjoy how easy it is to keep track of their assignments and announcements, the instant feedback on tests and some assignments, and the ability to ask questions when they need clarification. In a world where education is always changing and time is valuable, Google Classroom could be the answer that schools need to get the work done without all the stress and wasted time.

# Conclusion

Google Classroom may have a lot of competition in the market, but this does not mean it can't hold up against the rest. Classroom combines a lot of your favorite Google apps into one to help make it easier than ever to create lesson plans, send out assignments, provide feedback to students in real time and sometimes immediately, and to alert your students of any notifications and announcements that are important to the class. Teachers will find that it makes their teaching more effective with all the options and can save them a lot of time.

Students can use Classroom to easily complete assignments, ask any questions that they have, read announcements and participate in any of the discussions or group work that is required. With a valid Gmail address and an invitation from the teacher, it is easier than ever to get the work done and have all that information in one place.

This guidebook spent some time looking at the different aspects of Google Classroom, both from the perspective of the teacher and the student. Both groups are going to love all the options that open up with Classroom and how easy this platform is to use. Read through this guidebook to learn everything that you need for the ease of use and features of Google Classroom and learn why this is one of the best education platforms available today!